Prophetic Evangelism: Is the Church Ready for the new move of God?

A look at the styles of sharing the Christian faith throughout the History of the Church

By: Anna La Tona

ISBN: 978-1-475-23089-5

Printed in the United States of America

All Scripture references, unless otherwise specified, are taken from the New International Version.

Published by Holy Tapestry Ministries

DEDICATION

To my parents, who know me the best, and have been with me through the worst.
Thank you for your dedication throughout the years.

All my love to:
Jesus.... Forever!

Special Thanks to:

Live the Dream Team

Sylvia L Jones, Editor and Chief

Heavens Invasion Leadership Team for all the

encouragement and prayers

IHOP EG Prophetic team for your love and support

Pastor Gary Fishman and friends from the Bronx;

Russ Painter for all his help and devotion

Amelia Gomez, Liz Marasco, Phyllis Kibe,

Shefronica Gavin, Helga Becker, Ann Dillion

and the IHOP Prayer team

Sandy Alarcon...for all the laughs

Friends from King of Kings, and Harvest Training Center; Special friends from Texas: Shawn

Martin, and Ron Guidry; The Padians...love ya Paulie; My sister, Laura Reimer;

My 'techie' friends and support team: Evan F. and Henry Yang

TABLE of CONTENTS

TABLE of CONTENTS (cont.)

FOREWORD

Upon meeting Anna, it doesn't take long to discover her heart for the spiritually lost. She burns with a passion for seeing the Church take the fire, power and anointing of God, out into the streets, parks, malls, coffee shops, schools, businesses and anywhere else there is a single person separated from the arms of a loving Heavenly Father. Anna truly understands the Lord's command to "go and make disciples" (Matthew 28:19) which has proven through the ages to be a far more fruitful strategy, than sitting and waiting for the lost to walk into a Church building.

In the New Testament, revival was not something that was contained within endless Church meetings. Many of the miracles and moves of the Holy Spirit happened as the believers left their comfort zones and went out to be among the sinners. Jesus Himself was called a "friend of sinners" because of His propensity for hanging out with people who were seen as the riff-raff of society. While the religious crowd saw these tax collectors, prostitutes and down and outers as failures who were unworthy of their attention, Jesus looked at them through the eyes of faith, mercy and compassion. He saw in them the possibility and potential they were created to walk in and called it out of them.

That is the heart of prophetic evangelism. It doesn't take the revelation of the Holy Spirit to look into the eyes of a homeless person or a drug addict and prophecy back to them their sins and failures. Prophetic evangelism is not at its heart berating a messed up person for having ruined his or her life. Rather it is all about seeing others through Jesus' eyes. I have looked into the darkened hearts of gang members and envisioned by the Holy Spirit pastors, lawyers, and business men. In the same way the Prophet Ezekiel stared at a field of dry, dead bones and envisioned a mighty army (Ezekiel 37).

While spiritual gifts are powerful and needed within the body of Christ to minister to the needs of the saints, there is a hurting world out there whose only real hope may be you and other believers like you. This book is a challenge to take your gifts outside of the Church meetings because Jesus said "Lift up your eyes, and look on the fields; for they are white already to harvest. " (John 4:35) Having ministered with Anna and her team in many different non – Church settings, I have witnessed firsthand the power of God manifest in the hearts and bodies of the least likely people. Through supernatural healings, prophetic words of encouragement and the love of God softening hearts hardened by abuse, sin and rejection I have been a witness to many people who might never darken the door of a Church building being powerfully touched and at times overwhelmed by God's Presence.

While some may discard prophecy, healing, dream interpretation and other supernatural ministry as an unneeded relic of a long bygone era, there is no time in history where these gifts are needed more than today. I pray that this book would be a tool in your hands to discover the power and heavenly revelation that resides in you as a child of the King. Jesus sent out the 12 and then the seventy-two into the towns and cities of Israel with this charge: *Go and announce to them that the Kingdom of Heaven is near.[8] Heal the sick, raise the dead, cure those with leprosy, and cast out demons. Give as freely as you have received!* (Mark 10:7-8) 2,000 years later there is a commissioning from the Lord Jesus to go and do likewise in your own communities. The price of not heeding the call is a generation lost to the false gods, idols and distractions of this world. Anna and others the Lord is raising up with the same heart are not willing to let that happen, no matter the cost. Read this book not only as a source of good information but as a challenge from the very heart and mind of God.

Gary Fishman

Gary Fishman is the Associate Pastor of Sanctuary Fellowship, Bronx, New York. He has written two books: Dream Interpretation *and* Distorted Images of God's Heart: Pharisees in the Modern Day Church

INTRODUCTION

I remember just coming to know Christ and reading a book called, "Out of the Salt Shaker and into the World". It was written by a woman named Rebecca Manley Pippert. That was around 31 years ago. After I read the book I remember saying to myself, "I want to be an evangelist too!" I guess what really intrigued me was that the author of the book was a woman and was recognized as an Evangelist. In the year 1979, that was a pretty unique role for a woman in a church setting. Being a Christian woman and writing a book about her passion really interested me. We had a lot in common; we loved to speak to people about God, and we're both female. There were not many women who were really respected as leaders in the church in those days. I did not see many women taking on a leadership role in the church that I attended. The only woman I met in the church that were leaders, were Sunday school teachers. Usually the pastor's wife was the leader of a women's group and the role of the women's group was to make crafts, booties for babies and baked goods for the purpose of fund raising. If you were a single woman (not to mention prophetic), desiring to be a leader in a church setting was even more unique.

There seemed to be so many unwritten rules about being a female leader, especially being a single female leader. I don't think I ever discussed my feelings about this role of leadership. I just talked to God about it. He seemed fine with my idea of being a leader. Little did I know that He pre-destined me to be a leader - one that would lead many to Christ over a period of thirty years. My call, as I know it now, is not only to lead others to Christ, but equip saints for the purpose of ministry. Some churches still have trouble with women being leaders. Some churches still cannot get passed the fact that God is using the prophetic and power gifts and partnering them with evangelism. I say Prophetic Evangelists are here to stay!

The good news is that this is a time in which God has shifted His *Church* out of the four walls. The lost will be found in a way that the *church* would never have dreamed of. This book is a teaching tool which includes the testimonies of many people being led to the Lord through God's power and prophetic gifts. In it, you will read about certain methods that were used to bring others to Christ throughout church history and are still used today. It includes factors that hindered the church from bringing others to Christ. This book is not just for those who have the gift of evangelism, but for all who love the Lord and want others to know Him.

CHAPTER I

THE EVOLUTION OF PROPHETIC EVANGELISM

There are many factors historically that kept church members from evangelizing. Years ago, in many churches an evangelist was a man hired to share the Gospel. Outreaches were held in a church building or a tent. I never understood that. I asked myself, why would an evangelist come and speak to people in a church? To me an evangelist is a believer who goes out and finds divine appointments sent from the Holy Spirit. Divine appointments are opportunities for people to have a relationship with Christ. I always thought the meaning of the word 'evangelism' is to share your faith with unbelievers who are normally not connected to a church setting. I can imagine that some of you reading that last statement are saying to yourselves, "There are different types of evangelists." For me, an evangelist shares the faith outside the Church. Some Christians say that those who bring souls out of darkness are 'harvesters' and 'evangelists' has a different meaning... I don't know. The thing I do know is that we have made sharing our faith way too complicated.

OLD AND NEW STYLES AND METHODS OF EVANGELISM

Evangelism Explosion: Evangelism Explosion (E.E.) was and still is an evangelism tool which equipped churches to share the Gospel. It was popular in the late 1970's. Rev. D. James Kennedy was the founder of the tool. The style was unique, and required the learner to study Apologetics (Theological study, defending Christianity). The presentation dealt with most frequently asked questions concerning salvation. The Presentation includes bible verses that were specific to sharing the Gospel. E.E. training included role playing by trainers and trainees. The "script" or "presentation" used during role play was memorized by them. The trainers encouraged the trainees to present the Gospel in a way that could be clearly understood. If anyone had a question about the information presented, the trainers were able to answer the questions then move right back to the Gospel presentation. The goal was to lead people to the Lord and follow up with a visit and invitation to the church within a few days. One unique element about Evangelism Explosion was that it incorporated praying for the lost by having prayer partners. Prayer is such an important part of sharing our faith.

I was a trainee for awhile and I loved the way the team at our church took turns sharing their part of the Gospel. The presentation was awesome! The good thing about EE is that we learned bible verses that could be applied to our lives. The lessons on defending the Gospel aka the "Apologetics" as part of the presentation, was also a great tool. I've used the Apologetics over and over again in different situations.

Although Evangelism Explosion incorporated the bible, prayer, follow up and a dynamic presentation, most of the people who heard the presentation given by the E.E. team visited the church first. That is how the members of the team found people to talk to about salvation. One of the drawbacks to Evangelism Explosion was that the presentation was too long, plus it did not release the healing aspect of Holy Spirit or include the prophetic.

Friendship Evangelism: I understand that everyone has a unique style in sharing the Gospel message. Some people present the Gospel one on one. That's called Friendship Evangelism. Rebecca Pippert's book was one of the first books I read that was based on that style. In 1995, a book called, <u>Becoming a Contagious Christian</u> was out in print. It was written by Mark Mittelberg, Lee Strobel and Bill Hybels. The focus of the book was to develop an evangelism style that fit any believer for the purposes of sharing their faith. It is a great book.

The Friendship Evangelism style keeps the believer from being aggressive or even offensive. It eliminates the awkwardness of going up to someone whom you never met before and sharing something personal about God.

Tracts Evangelism: Handing out tracts is an adequate tool to sharing the gospel; however, tracts are not for everyone. Many styles of evangelism such as giving out tracts are considered pushy by some folks inside and outside of the church. Although many have come to know Christ through the Four Spiritual Laws, Chic Tracts and other tracts; it does not fit everyone's style of evangelism.

Servitude Evangelism (Example: Handing out Water): Our church has handed out more water than any church I know. It is the servant style of evangelism that shows that Christ was kind and that He loves to serve. The only drawback to Servitude Evangelism is that it does not show the side of God that is powerful - The Holy Spirit…The Healer. One of the names of God is Healer in the Old Testament. If you are in need of physical healing how does receiving a bottle of water meet the need? In John, chapter 14, Jesus said, "Greater works shall you do because I go to the Father." What is so great about handing out water? He said we would do greater works because He was going to the Father. We want to do the greater works that Jesus talks about in the bible! The kind of works that rely on God's awesome power! Handing out bottles of water does not require a reliance on God. Any unbeliever can hand out water to a stranger, but the greater works are to heal the sick and demonstrate the power of God to the lost.

-GOD IS SHIFTING

My desire to lead people to Christ one on one and encourage others to do the same never ceased. I have the same passion of leading to Christ now as I did 25 years ago. But the real question I've asked over the years was, "When do I get to do the stuff?" What I meant by that was I thought evangelism was sharing one on one with people using supernatural gifts. Then, in 2005 while praying, I remember feeling God say that it was time to take what I know about Him outside the walls of the Church. I did not think much of the impression at the time. Looking back, it was a turning point to my life. The rest of my days in ministry have been focused on sharing the gospel with a demonstration of the Holy Spirit and equipping others to do the same.

CHAPTER II

FORMAT VS. PERSONAL DESTINY

In the past, most gospel presentations focus on a format. This format is a memorized template which is shared with an unsaved person. It is like a "sales presentation". The presentation is intended to keep the person on track so they 'accept the Lord'. It's designed so that nothing keeps the person from finally saying the 'sinner's prayer'. If someone asks a question related to the Gospel, the answer is quickly given. If someone asks a question related to God, the answer is right there. The problem is not everyone is ready to accept the Lord at that time. We have to be sensitive to know when people are ready. The presentation is often rote, executed without thought. Jehovah Witnesses use this technique. The drawback to a rote presentation is people want real life answers to real life questions. They want to know about their destiny. People are concerned about their finances, they want to be encouraged, and they want a sense of security. People want physical healing along with the security of knowing where they go when they die. This can all be found through salvation through Jesus Christ. Paul wrote, "I did not come to you with persuasive words; but a demonstration of the Holy Spirit."

When we present a rote verbal discord to the lost, it does not show the uniqueness of Christ. Jesus Christ is unique because He cares about people's finances and their destinies. He protects and gives people security for this life and the one to come and that can be demonstrated through the Gospel presentation. Our old, routine presentation of the Gospel lacks an expression of who Christ is and only leads to vain arguments about religion. When people see the demonstration of the Spirit through healing it raises the level of faith to believe for increased finances and the like. It shows that God cares. When people see that God cares about them through a prophetic word or a destiny word, it leads them to believe for more. They can believe that God cares about their destiny, their families' destiny, and also have a sense that they can be protected and feel secure in knowing Jesus Christ.

-GOD HAS SHIFTED

God is doing a new thing. I'm not saying that we should neglect the use of the Word of God when we share. In fact, I want to reinforce God's Word. We should not neglect the apologetics aspect of sharing our faith either. However, God wants His power unleashed so that people have an experience of Him. <u>Just verbally sharing a memorized 'script' with people no longer cuts it.</u> Most people have heard enough. People want to see God move on their behalf. They want to know if God cares about them. Seldom have I read in the Word where Jesus asked for a commitment to Him before He demonstrates the Father's love through signs and wonders. Jesus demonstrated that the Father was a provider when he fed thousands of people at a time. It says that signs and wonders follow those who believe. The true evangelist is one who can tap in to the power of God and demonstrate the truth of the Gospel. The truth of the Gospel message speaks for itself. The truth is you can be healed, delivered and set free...That's GOOD NEWS!

The Gospel presentation is more than getting someone to say a prayer that gets them into heaven. When the Gospel is presented with signs and wonders, it shows the greatness of God. It tells us that God can meet people's needs. No religion can do that. People are robbed of the uniqueness, as well as the power of the cross when signs and wonders are not present. Christ, the sacrificial lamb, paid the price for our salvation which includes being healed, delivered and being set free.

We are witnesses to His supernatural power. It is hard to share something to others without experiencing it for yourself. How do I know that God speaks to others? He has spoken to me many times. How do I know that God heals? He has healed me many times. How do I know that God provides? He has provided for me. The only way we can present the Gospel with signs and wonders is to experience the supernatural ourselves.

CHAPTER III

PROPHETIC EVANGELISM NOW

Prophetic Evangelism is comprised of the gift of Prophecy and the gift of Evangelism. The Bible says, "We may all prophesy…"; in 1 Corinthians 14:31 and in 2 Timothy 4:5, it says to do the work of an evangelist. 1 Corinthians 12:10 also talks about the Gift of Prophecy as one (1) of the nine (9) supernatural gifts that the Holy Spirit gives us.

THE FOUR COMPONENTS

Prophecy is made up of four components: Revelation, Interpretation, Application and Declaration. Let's look at these components:

A. Revelation- God can reveal Himself any way He wants. He can reveal Himself to any one He wants to also. There are several examples in the Bible of God revealing Himself to unsaved men and woman. Just to name a few:

1. He spoke to a donkey in Numbers 22:21-39
2. He spoke to Pharaoh in a dream in Genesis 41:1-39
3. He spoke to Abimelech in Genesis 20:3-7 in a dream.
4. God spoke to the Midianite Soldier in a dream Judges 7:13-14
5. God spoke to Nebuchadnezzar in a dream in Daniel 2:1-4

Revelation can be from God's word. He can also reveal His heart in a song, which is sometimes called the Song of the Lord. The Song of the Lord can be impressed upon the heart of a person. It may be a song that everyone knows. It could be a church song or even a song that would be heard on a secular radio station. There are many other ways that people can hear God. Often God gives us an impression. The impression may come in a form of a pain in our body. This may be a clue that someone had a pain that needs to be healed. For example, I was in a prayer meeting and I had a pain in my knee. I said to the group that I was experiencing pain. Someone in the group was experiencing real pain in their knee and needed healing. When we prayed the person was healed immediately. What God reveals, He heals. God also uses visions and symbolic language to reveal Himself. God uses our sanctified imagination to reveal Himself in images that represent the things that are on His heart. When we have visions or dreams we are operating in the Seer Anointing which is part of the prophetic gift.

GIFT OF DISCERNMENT OF SPIRITS:

We explore the physical environment through our senses. God reveals Himself through our five spiritual senses so we can explore the spiritual realm. This is called the Gift of Discernment of Spirits (1 Corinthians 12:10). We will have a better understanding of this when we look at the Seer Anointing in the next chapter. God reveals Himself through nature, the Word and other ways. In the book of Acts, there are so many ways in which we see God revealing Himself. Take the example of Cornelius in Acts 10:1-4. He heard from an angel of the Lord. In Acts 16:16, Paul discerns that the slave girl, who had been following him, was possessed by the spirit of witchcraft. Jesus discerned that Nathanial had a good heart and had no guile in John 1:43-51. Jesus depended on His Father and used the supernatural gifts.

WORDS OF KNOWLEDGE:

Words of Knowledge are facts that the Holy Spirit shares with people in order to edify, encourage and enrich the people with whom those facts are connected. The gift of Word of Knowledge is listed in 1 Corinthians 12:8 "To one there is given through the Spirit a message of wisdom, to another a message of knowledge by means of the same Spirit" (NIV). It is a fact that would not be revealed about a person or thing unless God reveal it. For example, in Luke 5:4-11, *4Jesus says to Simon, "put out into deep water; and let down the nets for a catch." 5Simon answered, "Master. we worked hard all night and haven't caught anything. But because you say so, I will let down the nets." 6When they had done so, they caught such a large number of fish that their nets began to break. 7So they signaled their partners in the other boat to come and help them, and they came and filled both boats so full that they began to sink. 8When Simon Peter saw this, he fell at Jesus' feet and said, "Go away from me, Lord; I am a sinful man!" 9For he and all his companions were astonished at the catch they had taken, 10and so were James and John, the sons of Zebedee, Simon's partners. Then Jesus said to Simon, "Don't be afraid; from now on you will fish for people." 11So they pulled their boats up on shore, left everything and followed him.* If the Word of Knowledge and Gift of Discernment of Spirits is a good tool for **Jesus**, then it's a good tool for me! When we partner Evangelism with the Supernatural Gifts, we allow the Holy Spirit to have freedom, to convict (verse 8), to leave men astonished (verse 9) and make choices to leave the mundane and follow Christ (verse 11).

Here's an example of a Word of Knowledge. One day while getting for work, a thought popped up in my mind; it was 'silver shoes'. I went to work and I did not think of it all day until I went to my hair appointment. I looked at the hair dresser's shoes and the woman was wearing silver shoes. This is an example of receiving revelation for the purpose of evangelism. I knew she was the person that God wanted me to talk to. I had to ask myself, "What is God saying about the woman's silver shoes?" I was not sure what God wanted me to says, so I asked her if she had a dream I could interpret. She said she had a dream about her father. I interpreted the dream and it led her to ask questions about God. Later on I told her that God gave me an impression about a woman I would be meeting that day wearing 'silver shoes.' She was so impressed that she told so many others about our encounter. She ran all over the beauty salon telling everyone that God knew her and loved her! That is the way evangelism should work. If we have encounters with God, we can give others encounters with God. Then those people will tell others of His goodness. I did not have to share with the rest of the people in the hair salon. The woman with the silver shoes told everyone about our encounter.

JESUS, THE EVANGELIST:

In the New Testament, Jesus uses a Word of Knowledge to share with an unsaved woman at the well. As I previously stated, a Word of Knowledge is a fact that God reveals to a person. In the book of John 4:1-25, Jesus meets a Samaritan woman and begins to share with her. In John 4:16, Jesus asks the woman to call her husband. The woman replied that she had no husband. Jesus reveals that she had five husbands and the man that she was living with was not her husband either. She was astonished. She knew that Jesus heard from God. She responded by saying that Jesus must have been a prophet. In modern terms she would have said something like, "You must be a psychic!" When I speak to a pre-saved person using my prophetic gifting people ask, "Are you psychic?" We, as the *church* should be giving the lost encouraging words from God. An encouraging word, a "Spiritual Reading" or "Destiny Word" is a prophetic word that can change someone's destiny. For example: I was going into a supermarket and God spoke to me. He said, "The woman in the store needs healing." This is a Word of Knowledge given by God for the purpose of healing. He was referring to the woman in my view. I walked up to her and introduced myself. I proceeded to ask her if she needed healing for pain in her body. She said, "Yes, I do." I said, "I really feel God wants to heal you." She was stunned. I asked her for permission to place my hand on her shoulder and pray. I placed my hands on her and the pain was gone. I then received an encouraging word for her. I said that her past financial burdens would soon be gone. This is a way to use spiritual gifts and minister to the lost. She did say, "Are you a psychic?" She asked me if I was a psychic because for many years the *church* withheld God given Spiritual Gifts from the world. When the *church* does not operate in the gifts of the Holy Spirit, they are not able to share with the lost the way God intends. This creates an opening for psychics to speak into lives. The *church* is the vehicle that God is using to reveal Himself. Many Christians are rising up and taking their places in the world and beginning to share what God is saying through the Prophetic Gifts.

MORE WAYS IN WHICH GOD SPEAKS:

There are more ways God speaks to people. His word says in Amos 3:7, "Surely the Sovereign Lord does nothing without revealing his plan to his servants the prophets" (NIV). The Church is the modern day prophetic voice that God is using. We are the Church, not a building, but a people. The people of God have the authority to change the atmosphere as we hear from Him. The New Testament prophets are His people according to 1 Corinthians 14:31 - it says that we may all prophesy. It takes depending on His voice to change people, cities, regions and nations. His sheep hear His voice and speak what He says. They pray what He shares with them. We may all prophecy after hearing Him speak. He is so creative. He speaks in different ways, in different seasons.

God can also speak through His Word, the Bible. A Bible verse may seem like it is popping up off the page of Scripture. This is called a **Rhema Word**. A Rhema Word comes when Holy Spirit highlights a scripture verse. The verse might be something God uses to reveal His truth concerning a situation. We receive God's wisdom about a situation through His word.

There are so many ways God speaks to us. God may place a song in your heart. He may give you a **Vision.** God is able to bring revelation through so many aspects of our lives. Often, we can receive **Impressions** from God. An Impression, or a "gut feeling" about something or a situation may spring up in you. I remember being in our prophecy rooms and I had a gut feeling about a woman. I felt like she suffered from depression. The word, "depression" was superimposed over her. After we shared with her, I asked her if she had a history of depression. She said she suffered from it for many years. Because of this impression from God, we were able to declare deliverance from depression over her life.

God could also release a **dream** into our hearts. That is another form of revelation. After we receive revelation we have to interpret the revelation. This is the second component of the gift of Prophecy.

B. Interpretation- After we receive revelation from God we have to ask ourselves, "What is God saying to me?" When we interpret the revelation God gives us we often need resources to help us interpret the revelation correctly, especially if the revelation is in symbolic language. There are many books written that can be used to interpret symbols, numbers and colors. They are listed under resources in this book. Some Christians believe that God cannot use modern day symbols to reveal himself. I assure you, if God could use a donkey to speak in the Old Testament, He can use modern day objects and everyday language to speak to us. This is why it is important to have a cleansed mind. A renewed mind is necessary so God can share with us what is on <u>His</u> mind.

God uses symbolic language to reveal His heart. It is important to know the heart of God. He speaks to us through His Word and we can interpret what He is saying. Let me give you an example of an object that is not in the Bible. A car can be seen in a Dream or Vision. Dreams and Visions are part of the Seer Anointing. Let's say I had a vision that my car was going backward in my dream. In symbolic language a car represents ministry in some cases. Let's interpret that part of the dream. If my car represents my ministry, that would mean that it is losing ground and going backward in some way. When someone has a vision or dream, it may require more time to interpret. God will give us the interpretation. This does not mean we don't have to practice interpreting dreams. We have to develop the skill of interpreting visions as we wait and listen to God.

C. Application- One of the trickiest parts of prophecy is applying all the information God is sending us. You have to ask the question, "What do I do with the revelation that I am getting?" Not all information that God reveals should be shared. We have to ask God if he wants us to share the revelation or just use the revelation to pray about what He shares with us.

D. Declaration- If God says that we should share with others we have to share in the same tone as He is speaking. People often speak what God is saying as if He is angry. We must represent God as He truly reveals himself to us. We can share what God has given us through song, dance, mime, art, sign language or write it down and send it out. Declaring Jesus to the unsaved requires us to use non church language. We have to use common everyday words when we share our faith. See Chapter 6-The Importance of Presenting the Gospel Message, on how to not talk Christianese.

CHAPTER IV

The Seer Anointing

One of the questions we have to ask ourselves is "What is the Seer anointing?" The Seer anointing is part of the Prophetic gift. There are two types of prophetic people – Nabiy and the Seer. The Nabiy receives revelation through hearing and then share what they have heard in a *bubbling up* fashion. The Seer receives revelation in the form of images. People who have an anointing to be a Seer generally have more visions and dreams. They are, however, less spontaneous when they share what God is showing them.

Seers receive revelation through their senses. Our Spiritual sense of taste, touch, smell, seeing, and hearing can all be trained to determine the source of the revelation. Your spirit-man can distinguish and discern the sources of revelation. God can share what is in the human spirit also. The human spirit is made up of the mind, will and emotions. For example: I can recall a time when I was ministering in the prophetic rooms at a particular church. One of the ministers saw an image of a teddy bear. I was the leader in the prophetic rooms that night but did not know what the vision meant to the woman to whom we were ministering. I was about to make an attempt at sharing what I thought the teddy bear meant when all of a sudden the woman to whom we were ministering began to cry. She said, "I know the teddy bear is symbolic of my granddaughter." She explained to us that her granddaughter was sick and she holds onto a teddy bear when she does not feel well. The woman said, "I know the revelation came so I could pray for her". I would not have thought that was the interpretation, but as a team we included the four components of prophecy. The revelation was a teddy bear, the interpretation was related to the woman's kin and she applied the revelation by praying for her kin. It is as simple as that.

MORE SCRIPTURE RELATED TO DISCERNMENT OF SPIRITS

An example determining the motive of the heart is seen in Acts 14:8-9. Paul saw that a man had faith to be healed... *In Lystra, there sat a man who was lame. He had been that way from birth and had never walked. He listened to Paul as he was speaking. Paul looked directly at him, saw he had faith to be healed and called out, "stand up on your feet!" At that, the man jumped up and began to walk* (NIV).

Acts 5:1-7 is an example of discerning the motive of a person's heart...*Now a man named Ananias, together with his wife Sapphira, also sold a piece of property. With his* wife's full knowledge he kept back part of the money for himself, but brought the rest and put it at the apostles' feet. Then Peter said, "Ananias, how is it that satan has so filled your heart that you have lied to the Holy Spirit and have kept for yourself some of the money you received for the land? Didn't it belong to you before it was sold? And after it was sold, wasn't the money at your disposal? What made you think of doing such a thing? You have not lied just to human beings but to God." When Ananias heard this, he fell down and died. And great fear seized all who heard what had happened. Then some young men came forward, wrapped up his body, and carried him out and buried him. About three hours later his wife came in, not knowing what had happened." (NIV)

In Acts 16:16, Paul determined that the slave woman was being used by the devil to harass him..."Once when we were going to the place of prayer, we were met by a female slave who had a spirit by which she predicted the future....She followed Paul and the rest of us, shouting, "These men are servants of the Most High God, who are telling you the way to be saved." She kept this up for many days. Finally Paul became so annoyed that he turned around and said to the spirit, "In the name of Jesus Christ I command you to come out of her!" At that moment the spirit left her" (NIV)... The enemy motivated her to harass Paul.

Determining the sources from which revelation comes is important. We determine the sources of revelation through spending time with God, spending time in God's word, praying and maintaining a holy life and spending time with godly people. Intimacy with God is the key to understanding the things of the Spirit.

Training is important. Hebrews 5:13-14 tells us we need to be trained...Anyone who lives on milk, being still an infant, is not acquainted with the teaching about righteousness. But solid food is for the mature, who by constant use have trained themselves to distinguish good from evil (NIV). In 1 Corinthians, we read that we prophesy according to our faith, we prophecy in part, we all have a piece of the puzzle, our motive is to encourage, to strengthen and to comfort. We encourage others to join our prophetic mentoring team so that we can function the way God has called in the Body of Christ to funcation.. 1 Corinthians 14:31 says we may all prophesy.

Biblical References: I want to give Biblical references to what I am writing. There are many references to Seers in the Old Testament:

1st Sam. 9:9 Formerly in Israel, when a man went to inquire of God, he used to say, "Come and let us go to the Seer" for he who is called a prophet now was formerly a Seer. This means the person sees visions or receives impressions but it does not mean the visions or impressions are from God. The visions and dreams could be from another source. In the passage the word prophet is Nabiy which means speaking a word or words of encouragement that can change lives and allow for growth.

2nd Sam 24:11 When David arose in the morning, the word of the Lord came to the Prophet Gad, David's Seer. Gad was a Seer that dedicated his gift to the Lord and was used as David's seer.

The Bible says we may all prophesy in 1 Corinthians, chapter 14. Holy Spirit gives all people opportunities to hear from God or see visions or discern that there are demons or angels in the room. Many people have gifts but not all operate out of the gift that is given by the Holy Spirit. This is why we must discern the source of the revelation. We have to ask questions – Is God the source of the revelation? If the source of the revelation is not God, where is the source coming from? We are all given the ability to sense the Holy Spirit. The gift varies. The New Testament Seers are people like us that experience a "gut feeling", a perception or impression about something. Some people experience open heaven type visions such as in the book of **Ezekiel 1:1** *In the thirtieth year, in the fifth month, on the fifth day of the month, as I was among the exiles by the Chebar canal, the heavens were opened and I saw visions of God* (ESV).

OUR FIVE SENSES AS THEY RELATE TO THE SEER GIFT:

1. **Hearing-** Part of the Seer anointing. The disciples waited in the Upper Room according to the book of Acts chapter 2. They heard the sound of the mighty rushing wind.

2. **Taste-** Part of the Seer anointing. Ezekiel 3:3 speaks about tasting a scroll that is sweet as honey and bitter also.

3. **Touch-** Often people feel a pain and associate it with another person's ailment. Sometimes people feel a tingling feeling and it may mean the presence of the Lord is in the room. In Daniel 8:18, Daniel was touched and raised to his feet. Jesus felt someone touch him in Luke 8:43-46. It was the woman with the issue of blood. He would have had to discern that he was being touched by her because there were many people trying to touch Him that day. In Isaiah 6:7, Isaiah was touched with coal.

4. **Smell-** Jesus is the Rose of Sharon. Sometimes people will sense a fragrant that is from heaven. I smelled the dew of heaven in church one day. 2 Corinthians 2:14 *But thanks be to God who always leads us into triumphal procession in Christ and spreads everywhere the fragrance of the knowledge of Him.* (NIV)

5. **Seeing-** In the book of Acts 10:9, Peter fell into a trance and experienced a vision of four footed animals and heard the voice of God saying, *"Get up, Peter, kill and*

eat." In Acts 16:9, Paul had a vision of a man of Macedonia standing and begging him to come to Macedonia.

THE SEER GIFT AND EVANGELISM

We incorporate the Seer anointing when we share the message of the Gospel. I was talking to a man in the Bronx one day and I saw a vision of a heart that was broken. I asked him if his heart was broken. He said he just broke up with his girlfriend and his heart was indeed broken.

The Treasure Hunt and the Woman at the Mall

Our team went to the mall at Christmas time. We used the Treasure Hunt approach to sharing our faith. The Treasure Hunt is a prophetic evangelism tool in which we receive words of knowledge and write those words on a paper called the Treasure Map. The Treasure Map includes: a space for a location to meet divine appointments, a space for an ailment someone may have, a space for a person's name, something that they are wearing, and something unique. The tool was introduced through a book called The Ultimate Treasure Hunt, by Kevin Dedmon. He is from Bethel Church in California. So with our Treasure Map, our team headed out and did an outreach at a local, crowded mall in New Jersey. We prayed and God began showing us where to go and the physical ailments that we would encounter. A woman matched the description that was written on our Treasure Map. We had an ailment of a "shoulder injury" listed on our treasure list. This was great - we found our treasure! We approached her and asked her if she needed prayer. She said, "Is it free?" We said, "Yes!" Then, we asked her if we could touch her shoulder. She said her shoulder hurt and she could no longer carry her bags through the mall. We began to pray and she began to feel heat. Heat, is a physical indication that God is healing the part of the body where that heat is felt. The pain was gone within minutes and she was moving her arm. The woman started to proclaim the name of Jesus. We were not sure she was a Christian but she began to scream "Praise the Lord!" People in the store watched as the power of God healed this woman. We were excited! This is just one of the many testimonies of the power of God.

We found Charlie in the Bronx

The same thing happened in Bronx, New York. Our team did a Prophetic Evangelism outreach there. The name Charlie was on the Treasure Map list. 'Cancer' was written on the list along with 'black leather jacket'. The group found a man named Charlie. He said he had been looking for someone to pray for his wife who had Cancer. He wore a black leather jacket. The group went to his house and prayed for his wife. That is what I mean about divine appointments.

We found Stephanie

Now, the first time I went to a meeting where the Treasure Hunt Evangelism tool was being used, I was skeptical. The first name we had on our Treasure list was Stephanie. We felt like our location would be Dunkin Donuts on the south bound lane of Route 17 in Bergen County, New Jersey. We set out to find Stephanie but there was no one there by that name. We asked the woman in the store if she had a dream we could interpret instead. After interpreting the dream, we led the woman in prayer to accept Christ as her Savior. After that encounter, we set out to find Stephanie at another Dunkin Donuts on the other side of the high way. The team walked in and asked if a Stephanie was there. Sure enough, Stephanie was there. From that moment on, I was hooked on the Treasure Hunt Style of Evangelism. We have been doing Treasure Hunts ever since.

The Woman in Supermarket

I discerned the spirit of Witchcraft when speaking to a woman I met at a supermarket. It was the same spirit that Paul the Apostle experienced in Acts 16:16. I saw a dark cloud over her and I asked the woman if she engaged in Tarot card readings. She said, "Yes." She also said that she began to experience seeing dark shadows following her and she became fearful so she stopped reading Tarot cards. I told her that she could repent and ask God to come in to her life and be free of fear. This is an example of Discernment of Spirits.

A Woman with Cancer in Her Blood Line

I went up to a woman in the mall and I had an impression that she had cancer in her generational blood line. I discerned that there was cancer in her family. She confirmed that there was indeed cancer in her family. This is an example of the use of the Seer gift. Discerning of Spirits can be used as a tool for deliverance. Salvation through Jesus Christ includes healing, deliverance and being set free from all bondage. I prayed for her and bound up cancer in her life. Remember the scripture says "Whatever you bind on earth is bound in heaven; whatever you loose on earth is loosed in heaven."

This is example of using the authority that Christ gives us to release people from captivity of illness. According to Isaiah 61:1, the Spirit of the Sovereign Lord is upon us because He has anointed us to bring Good News. We are the ones who bring the Good

News. The Good News is that anyone who calls upon the Lord can be saved. This passage tells us that through Jesus we can release others out of all kinds of bondage. We, the Body of Christ have been anointed not just to share the Good News verbally, but demonstrate His power outside of the four walls of the church. There are many testimonies written by the Live the Dream Prophetic Evangelism team that are examples of the use of the Seer anointing to reach the lost. You can read about them in Chapter 7- Testimonies.

IMPRESSIONS AS PART OF THE SEER GIFT:

An impression does not always come with an image. It may is a hunch or a gut feeling. Many traditional churches have dismissed a lot of revelation simply because they do not believe that God speaks through impressions, pictures, symbols, colors, or numbers. They have dismissed the demonstration of the power of the Supernatural because of unbelief.

You may experience an impression, or see a snap shot picture of a person with whom God wants you to share. You may receive a snap shot picture in your mind of a body part God wants you, or your team of prophetic evangelists, to pray for. I received a vision that was like watching a movie of a person's life. At that point, I had to decide what to do with the vision God was giving me. It was a vision of someone's stomach. I was a missionary in the Dominican Republic and asked the person, through a translator, if they had stomach problems. The man said his stomach was in pain. We prayed and he was healed.

These are a few examples of Prophetic Evangelism. There are more examples in Chapter 7- Testimonies. Remember when you receive any revelation to go back to the lesson on the components of prophecy written in Chapter 3-Prophetic Evangelism Now.

Remember to ask, " Is God saying something? " Does God want me to share what he is telling me with others?" "Does He want me to pray about what I saw?" We will learn more about how to share the revelations we receive from the Lord later when we speak about the importance of sharing the Gospel message.

CHAPTER V

Dreams as a Tool of Prophetic Evangelism

God uses dreams to speak to people. God can speak to someone who knows Him, or He can speak to someone who does not know him. In Genesis 20:3-7, God spoke to Abimelech. He was the King of Gerar and did not know God as Abraham did. This was a warning dream.

THE PURPOSE OF DREAMS

There are many purposes to dreaming. God wants to get our attention. He may not have our full attention during the day, but He can speak to us during the night in a dream. Job 33:14 says that God speaks not only once, but more than once, even though men do not regard it (Amp). Dreams that are from God can give us clear direction, they can warn us or call us into intercession or spiritual warfare. Dreams can bring us to our destiny or clarify our calling. Some people have been healed through their dreams. Some people have had dreams in which they invented something that was life changing. Remember, dreams and visions are part of the gift of Prophecy and they are for the purpose of strengthening, encouraging and comforting believers as well as unbelievers, according to 1 Corinthians 14:3.

INTERPRETING DREAMS

Interpreting dreams is another tool to share our faith and is a great way to reach lost people. It is a Prophetic Evangelism tool that anyone can use after being trained. I was taught dream interpretation through Streams Ministries. What an awesome tool! It's been great teaching groups of people to interpret dreams also. Dreams are a part of being a Seer. Every prophetic person can learn to be a dream interpreter through learning, and practicing the skill of dream interpretation.

DREAM PARTIES

Dream Parties are fun. One night we invited friends to our house for a dream interpretation party. Everyone joined in sharing their dream. Inviting friends, neighbors and family over for a dream interpretation night is inexpensive. Many people come to know Christ at Dream Parties.

LITERAL DREAMS

God may give someone a dream and the dream actually happens in real life. Many years ago I met a woman who had dreams that would occur the same exact way as she described in the dream. Some of the dreams had good outcomes and some of them did not. I always encouraged her to pray and seek God so that the dreams that were negative would turn around for the good.

INTERCESSORY AND SPIRITUAL WARFARE DREAMS

God uses dreams to reveals the strategies of the enemy. God can lead us to pray against enemy attacks as well as call us to pray for one another or a situation. The following are scripture references that show us examples of types of dreams:

1. **Warning dreams**- Dreams that warn you concerning danger or attacks of the enemy. He uses these dreams to show us the results of our actions. Genesis 20:1-7.

2. **Destiny dreams**- Reveal the passion in our hearts for the thing God is calling us to do. Gen 28:11-15

3. **Direction dreams**- Give us direction or instructions concerning the things in our lives. Matthew 2:1-20.

4. **Healing dreams**- Sometimes God actually heals us physically or emotionally in our dreams. Isaiah 61 and Luke 4:18, shows us that God came to set us free and heal us. A woman from a local church said that she had a dream that she was healed of cancer in her dream. God can do anything.

5. **Conviction dreams**- This is a type of dream in which God convicts a person of sin. Job 33:17

6. **Future dream**- In Daniel 7:1-2, God revealed the future to Daniel. God can use a dream to reveal his future to us.

7. **Wisdom dreams**- A dream that encourages the believer to gain wisdom: God gave Solomon a dream that gave him insight and wisdom in 1st Kings 3:5-15.

ORGANIZING YOUR DREAMS

Some people dream a lot. It helps to keep them organized by placing them into a binder with tabs. Each tab represents a category or type of dream. For example, I put all my spiritual warfare dreams behind the tab labeled 'Spiritual Warfare'. I organize it according to the date of the dream. When I go back to that date I can recall what was going on in my life in that particular season. I usually include a title to the dream such as: <u>The Spider Dream</u>. I write briefly about the people in the dream as well as where the dream took place. Giving a title and brief summary of the dream helps the dreamer recall what the dream is about. It may take time to figure out the dream. Sometimes I call other Dream interpreters. Some people keep a journal by their bed so when they awake, they can write them down. It may be hard to write the dream down clearly especially when you are very tired or just woke up. I ask other dream interpreters for their input into dreams. Since we prophecy in part and see in part, we need input from others.

SOURCES OF DREAMS

There are various sources of dreams. The Lord can be the source of a dream. The enemy could also be a source of a dream by releasing fear, depression and oppression; leaving the dreamer feeling hopeless. We can have dreams that come from our soul. Our soul is made up of the mind, will and emotions. They are called soulish dreams. In soulish dreams, we play out our feelings of the stress we have experienced during the day. God can use all our dreams for His purpose. Some dreams help us to resolve the conflicts that we are experiencing during the day.

DREAMS AS THEY RELATE TO SHARING WITH THE LOST

God said he would pour out his Spirit on all flesh in the book of Joel. He fulfilled the promise in the New Testament in Acts 2:16-21. It says, 'But this is what was spoken by the prophet Joel, "And it shall come to pass in the last days, says God, that I will pour out My Spirit on all flesh; your sons and daughters shall prophecy, your young men shall see visions, your old men shall dream dreams. And on My menservants and on My maidservants I will pour out My Spirit in those days and they shall prophecy." When He said that He would pour out His Spirit, He meant unsaved people as well as saved people. Here's an example of the outpouring of the Holy Spirit and the use of dreams to reach the lost: Our team met a woman in a Dunkin Donuts. She had a dream about her father. I could see that the symbol of her earthly father related to her heavenly Father. She was able to understand Father God's love for her. She was asked by a team member if she would like to pray and ask Jesus to come into her life. She agreed and wanted to ask Jesus to be her Savior. This is an example of using a dream to bring Salvation to the lost. As a result of her salvation she experienced the Father's love for her.

CHAPTER VI

The Importance of Presenting the Gospel Message

MEET PEOPLE WHERE THEY'RE AT SPIRITUALLY.

One Summer I was in Times Square, New York, during a Prophetic Evangelism outreach. I was with another team member when we met a believer from a church in the Times Square area. She was handing out flyers to attract people to attend a play in New York City; this was her job. She was working with another employee who did not have the same faith in God. We approached them and asked if either of them had a dream. The woman who did not have a relationship with the Lord said, "I had a dream that I was going up higher and higher into the sky." I felt like she really desired to come up to a higher level in her spiritual experience and know God. Then it happened. Her co-worker, who was a believer started to download the do's and don'ts of Christianity in rapid fire. She began saying. "If you were to die today and did not accept Christ, you would not go to heaven." That is true, but the unsaved co-worker was so filled with confusion she became afraid. This is what I call 'Putting the Cart before the Horse' style of evangelism. It is really an old approach to sharing with the lost. Some believers want to seal the deal and ask for a commitment to Christ instantly. People have to be met where they are at spiritually when it comes to presenting the Gospel message. When we share too much information it is like giving steak to a baby. Eventually, the baby will choke.

TESTIMONIES ARE IMPORTANT

The best way to present the Gospel is simply telling others of your experience with God. Many Christians can't share about Jesus because they have not experienced a deep relationship with Him. You cannot share about someone if you do not know them. If your relationship with Jesus is shallow, your testimony will be shallow too.

CONVEY THE RIGHT WORDS WITHOUT SOUNDING OVERLY SPIRITUAL

Using words that people can understand to communicate the Gospel message is important. Very often, believers use the same language with their unsaved friends and family as they do in church. It is difficult for the unsaved person to understand what they are talking about. It leaves them confused. Author, Teacher and Prophetic Evangelist, Doug

Addison, wrote a little pamphlet called, <u>No More Christianese</u>. It is a guide to sharing our faith using words that everyone can relate to. It aids the believer in eliminating religious words so the unsaved person can understand the Gospel message. Many Christians mention that an unsaved person must be born again. Being born again can mean a number of things depending on who you are speaking with. I've read about many famous people who said they were born again, but their lives did not reflect the Christ that I know. Before I was a Christian, I read bumper stickers that said "Jesus saves." I wondered what He saved. It raised many questions in my mind.

Let's talk about words that can be considered 'religious'. These are religious clichés that Christians use on a consistent basis. For example, the word **anointing** is a word commonly used by Christians. According to the Oxford Dictionary, the word anointing means: to spread oil on something. Unsaved people hearing about the **anointing** may wonder what the word anointing means. If I were unsaved, I'd like to know why oil is being spread upon me. We, as believers can use another word to convey the meaning of anointing. I would use the word anointing in a sentence and say, "God is giving you **special grace** to bring good things into your life and the life of others."

Another commonly used religious word is **mantle**. One meaning of mantle is: cover over, another definition is: a covering over a fire place. The word mantle does not seem like a word that a unbeliever would use based on those definitions. Christians talk about mantles over peoples' lives. If I were speaking to an unbeliever I would say, "There is something that God wants you to do. **He will be with you and guide you** so you will be able to fulfill it. Do not be afraid to get to know Him." I could explain how I came to know Him after sharing the encouraging word or Prophecy. Let's look at another common word that Christians might use when sharing their faith. I gave reference to the word **born again**. The only place where being " born again" is mentioned in the Bible is when Jesus shared with a man named Nicodemus. Telling an unsaved person they need to be born again does not convey the same message that Jesus was trying to convey to Nicodemus. We need to say something like" You can have a new start in your life when you ask God to meet you in your present circumstances.

Making Jesus real to others is the key to sharing. People want to know that they are loved. They will know that they are loved when someone can pinpoint their need and simply direct them to a life of freedom. Simplifying the presentation of the Gospel by using common words will give the unsaved person less to unscramble in their mind. When Jesus is revealed through the gifts, people's spirits awaken and become tuned in to what the believer is saying about God. When you are able to share spirit to spirit, many people will come to Christ and be set free. That is what the Gospel is about… setting people free; not wrangling over a bunch of words.

Using phrases such as being "born in sin" is difficult to explain to an unsaved person. I personally have to figure out what that means and I've been a Christian for 30 years. Christians believe that we are all born in sin. This is a true statement, but that would be a good lesson to follow up with in the word when the person finally receives Jesus. The goal is to direct people to the Savior. He cares about their financial needs and disappointments. Speak to the person's sadness and disappointments after using the gifts to waken their Spirit. This is what draws people to desire Jesus. There is a time and place to share deeper.

DO'S AND DON'TS TO APPROACHING OTHERS WITH THE GOSPEL

Do: Share from your heart. Believers and unbelievers alike can tell when people are sincere. When we present the Gospel message we are offering others a chance of a lifetime to meet Jesus. When we share our lives, people begin to open their hearts. The love of Jesus is so real, people will know there is something different about you. It opens doors for them to trust.

Do: Keep it real. Be yourself. No one can be you except for you. Share testimonies of His goodness the way you would share with a friend. A testimony raises the faith of unbelievers just as it does for believers. Share testimonies of your healing. Share testimonies of His faithfulness to provide for you. Share how He has gotten you out of a jam. Keep it light and keep it real.

Do: Present the Gospel Message clearly: After you have gotten the unsaved person's attention through an encouraging word (i.e.: an accurate word of prophecy like a Word of Knowledge) or the person was healed or you interpreted a dream, this is the time to present the Gospel clearly. Explain the Gospel from the word of God. Ask the person if you can share from the word of God. Go through the Romans Road (below), or explain John 3:16. Ask them if they feel they want to know Jesus. Through sharing your testimony, you can bring your experience of Jesus to the person. Present the Gospel clearly from the word:

1. **Romans 3:23, "For all have sinned and fallen short of the glory of God. "**
   If I were to share this verse with an unsaved person, I would say, **"No one lives up to God's standards."**

2. **Romans 5:8, "God demonstrates His love for us in that when we were sinners, Christ died for us."** This is a verse I would use after Romans 3:23. **I would simplify it by saying, "No one lives up to God's standards but God still loved**

us, so He took our place on the cross when He died for us. We really should have been the ones that died. Christ died for us instead."

3. **Romans 6:23, " For the wages of sin is death, but the gift of God is eternal life, through Jesus Christ our Lord."** This is a great verse which tells the unbeliever that it cost God the death of his Son because we did not live up to that standard that God set for us

4. **Romans 10:9, If, we confess with our mouth Jesus is Lord and believe in our hearts that God raised Jesus from the dead, you will be saved."** In other words, if you tell God you are sorry for not living up to the standards set by Him in heaven and believe that He died to meet those standards, you can be right with God.

Do: Follow up…it's important. If they accept the Lord; ask them to attend church with you. When we have outreaches that are out of town, I usually try to find a Bible believing church in which the newly saved person can attend. We use connect cards. The connect cards have a website on them. The newly saved person can go to the website and read about God. This is all part of following up on a new born Christian. I ask for their phone number or an e-mail address so we can keep in contact. Many believers share the Gospel, but do not have a way to follow up on the newly saved person. A follow up program should be in place before sharing the Gospel.

Do: Practice receiving and giving words of knowledge, healing and dream interpretation with a team of people. Practice is important when it comes to the prophetic. Find a prophetic group of people or attend a prophetic conference in your area. If you are in the New York, New Jersey area, you can contact livethedeamtoo@comcast.net.

Do: Pray, pray, pray. You will not find divine appointments and encounters without praying. Prayer is the key to evangelism. Have intercessors pray for you before, during and after every outreach.

Do: Go out as a team. Teams of two or three should go out and share with a person. If there are too many people on the team it intimidates people. They may think you are trying to hurt, or scam them and they will walk away. Old people are usually fearful. Approach them, but be sensitive about getting into their space. Do explain who you are and what you are doing. Introduce yourself. State the obvious such as: **"My name is_____, I am learning how to interpret dreams, do you have a dream that we can interpret?"** If they do not have a dream, you can ask if they would like an encouraging word. Encouraging words should be presented clearly and accurately. All team members can take turns sharing. Another approach to sharing is to ask people who are obviously injured if they would like prayer to be healed.

Do: Be happy. People who know Jesus should be the happiest people on earth. Approach people with a smile and be yourself. Keep things light. If people sense you are fearful they will not trust that you have Good News to share with them.

Do: Be mindful of the Clothing and Jewelry you wear when sharing the Gospel. It can be a turn off to the lost folks when Christians wear religious clothing. Wearing shirts with Bible references makes no sense when presenting the Gospel. When a believer approaches an unsaved person with a Bible verse on their shirt, or a piece of jewelry that represents a certain religion, the unsaved person already has an preconceived idea of what kind of encounter they may experience. If they have had a bad experience with meeting Christians, they may associate you with that person they met in the past.

DON'T: Overload People. Be sensitive. Listen to people. Read their body language. If they are not interested in what you are saying, thank them for their time and politely walk away. The reason why the Treasure Hunt, Dreams, and Prophetic Evangelism is so important is it is that they are keys to reaching people in this season. If you don't get someone's attention and connect with them, it makes it hard to speak to them about the Gospel.

Sharing our faith by Keeping It Real: There comes a point where the Gospel message needs to be presented clearly. Many people explain the Romans Road (Romans 10:9) to the unsaved.

Approaches to the Gospel using Power Evangelism: Power Evangelism is a tool that gets a person's attention. Believers often say that the person needs to be a believer before they can get healed. Jesus healed many people instantly, and then they became believers. Jesus acknowledged that the woman with an issue of blood needed healing. There were so many people who could have touched Him that day, but I believe that God the Father encouraged Jesus to sense that particular woman needed healing that day. Example: One Sunday, a woman we met in New York was instantly healed as we shared. She and her whole family came to Christ and began attending a local church that next Sunday. Power Evangelism is a release of the Holy Spirit on an unbeliever to attract them to Jesus. That is Good News!

Jesus was the perfect evangelist. He got the attention of the woman at the well through a Word of Knowledge. I've met people who prophesy over tattoos and body piercings. This is the way they get the attention of the lost. They are 'meeting them where they're at'. After that, they present the Good News. If you share your faith without getting the person's attention, you're leaving out the most important aspect to the Gospel presentation, Jesus. Jesus IS the Good News.

SPECIAL NOTE: I mentioned that prayer is the key to evangelism. There are different ways of praying for the lost. God may give us a strategy in prayer specifically on how to reach the lost. God may want us to pray and ask for souls and divine appointments. The key to sharing the Gospel is being intimate with God. Knowing God's heart leads us to a deeper desire to see the lost come to Him. When we have divine encounters, we desire for those around us to also experience Jesus. I challenge those reading this book to become intimate with God through worship and spending time with Him. Bill Johnson, pastor of Bethel Church in Redding, California, says that "evangelism is an over flow of worship". I guarantee those reading this book will have a greater desire to see others encounter Him.

CHAPTER VII

Testimonies

My team has been doing Prophetic Evangelsim outreaches for years. We started with a dream team called 'Live the Dream.' I trained many people to interpret dreams. I came to realize that it takes time to be accurate with dreams. Many of the team members come from Spirit filled churches, but never had the chance to witness the power of God working through them; bringing forth healing, especially healing outside the four walls of the church. The team has been a blessing to me and here are some of their testimonies:

Debbie's Evangelism Testimony
(This is an example of Prophetic Evangelism)

Debbie has been a member of Live the Dream Team for many years. We were at the mall and Debbie saw a man with a brace on his knee. She received a Word of Knowledge and told the man he had a torn ligament. It was true. He did have a torn ligament. The man was very opened to hearing what Debbie had to say after that. She continued receiving visions about things that went on in his childhood. He knew that God was speaking to him after talking to Debbie. He began to believe that God was speaking and was in control of the things in his life.

That same afternoon at the mall, Debbie met a woman and her daughter. Before she introduced herself to them she had a Word of Knowledge. The word was tumors. She went up to the woman and said, I believe that your daughter has tumors. Her daughter did have tumors. The mom put Debbie's hand on her daughter's shoulder and she felt a missing piece in that shoulder area. It had been removed surgically because she had a tumor. She was stunned and began to cry when Debbie said her daughter had more tumors in her body. Debbie asked her if she could pray and release healing to her daughter.

Eddie's Testimony
(This is an example of a Treasure Hunt experience)

The youth group from a local church had a lot of successes with Treasure Hunts and Eddie is one of those members. Here's his Evangelism Testimony: "One Saturday morning I had 'yellow shirt and pink shirt' written down under the topic: Appearance on the Treasure Hunt Map. I went down street with my team and we saw a woman wearing a bright yellow shirt. We approached her. A man with a pink shirt was with her. I explained to them that God highlighted them that day and I showed them that I had 'pink shirt and yellow shirt' written on my Treasure Map. We prayed for them about an apartment they were looking for.

On a different day, our team went out for another Treasure Hunt experience. I wrote down 'Hawaiian shirt' and the name 'Mary' on the Treasure Map. I saw a woman across the street that looked like she was wearing a Hawaiian shirt. My team waited and the woman came across the street. The team prayed for her. We realized her name matched the name we had for her on our Treasure Map."

Scott's Evangelism Testimony

A group of 12 traveled to New Jersey to meet some friends (mostly youth) from a church located in Bronx, New York. There were about 25 of us asking the Holy Spirit for clues to find His treasure. A few of the many prophetic clues we received were: local park, paralyzed, drinking problem, the name John or Juan, the number 18, and the name Mike. Five or six of the members had a sense of the Lord wanting to heal a knee, someone saw a vision of crutches, someone else 'heard the words', it hurts, it hurts. We had a number of other clues. We went out in groups of 3. Hector was with me, an enthusiastic young leader, was with me. We shared and prayed with a few people on our way to the park. Hector was getting excited. Up ahead he saw a man with a cane who could barely walk. He had an ace bandage on his knee.

I took the lead on this (took the position of being the lead person to pose questions to the lost, usually each team member takes a turn doing this), and we discovered David. He was the man with the cane who had been to Bible School, but wasn't currently serving the Lord. He recently injured his knee while jogging. We assured him that the Lord never stopped loving him and the He wanted to heal his knee as a sign of His love for him. David admitted that he had been drinking a little earlier, to relieve the pain. He then said, "It hurts, it hurts." Wow!!! I showed him where I had those very words of his already written on my Treasure Map!!! This encouraged our faith. As we were laid our hands on David and prayed for him, one thing I declared was peace to his knee, and soul. After praying, I asked him, "How do you feel?" He said he felt peace! Immediately he hung his cane on the fence behind him, put weight on his knee, and tested it, then declared, "I couldn't do that if you paid me!" Immediately, he began to power-walk down the sidewalk! He was exclaiming, "God healed my knee! Jesus healed me!" Hector was also excited and was literally leaping for joy and yelling out, "Jesus heals! Come here if you want prayer for healing!"

I heard later that simultaneously, the Lord was also healing someone's ankle. Also, I noticed a well-dressed man about 30 feet away, intently watching what was happening. He called some of our team over. He wanted to know who we were and what group we were with. He was deeply touched, because as it turned out, just that morning he had been in anguish, crying out to the Lord in prayer, "Why is it that although I read in the Bible about people being healed and saved in the streets, I never see it here and now?"

How gracious is the Lord to let us not only see, but to let us also partner with Him as He reaches out to those who are indeed His Treasure!"

CHAPTER VIII

Conclusion

The best evangelists are yet to be discovered. They are people who do not desire a title. They are those who hear the Father's call to bring in the lost. They are ordinary people from all walks of life. They are people who do not need the title Evangelist. They are ordinary people who look out their window and seek to touch those around them. They are people who see as the Father sees. People who love the way God loves. They are people who want to make a difference. They're prayerful people with a purposeful desire to share with friends, or strangers.

I wrote this book to show how evangelism has evolved in the Church. It's getting easier and easier to reach the lost. It's easy because there are no formulas. Evangelism is easy when we depend on the Father. When we listen to His voice and hear His cry for the lost we can bring in the harvest that He has ordained to bring forth. Depending on Him is the key. The rest is up to us to obey. Now, that is the real challenge!

NOTES

NOTES

_____

_____

_____

_____

_____

_____

_____

_____

_____

_____

AUTHOR'S BIOGRAPHY

Anna La Tona, a New Jersey native, is a graduate of Montclair State University, Kean University and Union County College. She obtained a degree in Occupational Therapy, Recreation and Physical Education, as well as a Master's certificate in Sports Medicine. Anna presently works with Autistic children, Asperger's Syndrome, and Attention Deficit Disorders in the public school system.

Anna attended Bible College and The Institute for Spiritual Development where she learned about dream interpretation and the prophetic gift. Thereafter, Anna founded the Live the Dream Ministry, a dream interpretation and prophetic evangelism regional ministry. Through dream interpretation, Treasure Hunt style of evangelism and power evangelism, Live the Dream Ministry has been changing lives in New Jersey areas as well as the five boroughs of New York City by way of monthly outreaches.

Anna has coordinated the Prophetic Intercession Church Ministry and has been an Overseer for 5 Fellowship Groups in Elizabeth, NJ. She has also served as a Sunday school teacher. Anna has been a leader on the Prophetic team and served on Breath of the

Spirit Dream team in Texas. She is presently a mentor to IHOP EG prophetic team and recently helped coordinate the prophetic team for the Mantle of Power conference in New Jersey. She is a teacher at Kingdom Training Institute. She teaches about the prophetic gifts, the Seer anointing, dream interpretation and prophetic evangelism.

She is aligned with Mantle of Power Ministry, Heavens Invasion Regional Ministry, FireSong Prophetic Worship Ministry and other local churches. Anna preaches also and has recently been asked to speak at the United Nations in New York City. There, she will encourage Gods people. Her goal is to strengthen and encourage others to come up higher where ever she goes.

RESOURCES:

Gary Fishman, <u>Dream Interpretation: A beginner's Manual and Dictionary</u>,
Ascribe Publishing

Doug Addison, <u>Christianese, In Light Connection Ministries</u>,
Fruit Bearer Publishers

Jim Goll, <u>The Seer</u>,
Destiny Image Publishers, Inc.

Rebecca Manley Pippert, <u>Out of the Salt Shaker and Into the World</u>,
InterVarsity Press

D. James Kennedy and T.M. Moore, <u>Evangelism Explosion</u>,
InterVarsity Christian Fellowship Press
Tyndale House Publishers

Mark Mittleberg, Lee Strobel, Bill Hybals, <u>Becoming A Contagious Christian</u>,
Zondervon Books

To contact Anna write to: livethedreamtoo@comcast.net
or go to her web page at: www.home.comcast.net/~livethedreamtoo/site/

Made in the USA
Charleston, SC
29 August 2013